Ready f

8 PROVEN STEPS TO GET YOUR DREAM JOB AS A
FLIGHT ATTENDANT

Believe in yourself

and the world

will follow your lead!

Xoxo,

Miss Kaykrizz

Miss Kaykrizz have written blog posts articles and created YouTube videos that helped inspire, encourage and give out practical tutorials for aspiring Flight Attendants to achieve their Dreams.

Aside from this book she just recently launched her Skype One-on-One Coaching to meet aspirants where they are and provide guidance on their FA applications.

Soon, she will be launching the first Online Flight Attendant School to provide courses that aims to prepare candidates that breaks barriers of time, location and price.

Visit www.misskaykrizz.com to book a coaching session now.

8 PROVEN STEPS TO GET YOUR DREAM JOB AS A FLIGHT ATTENDANT

MISS KAYKRIZZ

YouTube Personality and Blogger

www.misskaykrizz.com

Ready for Take-Off:

8 Proven Steps to Get your Dream Job as a Flight Attendant

MISS KAYKRIZZ

Cover Concept: John Paul Maclang
Cover Artist: Kevin Cachuela
Illustrations: Jerald Belgira

www.misskaykrizz.com

Table of Contents

Step 6: Emotional Preparation

Step 7: Spiritual Preparation

Step 8: Take Action to Land Your Dream Job

Dedication

First of all, To God be all the glory.
Everything I do is for the love and service of the Lord.

I dedicate this book to my Family.

I would like to thank specially my first cousin Kuya
Cheking for recognizing my love for writing and
encouraging me to be a writer. With that seed planted,
I am here now writing my first book.

To my Mommy Eva, who have always been my rock,
who supported me emotionally and financially, I love
you to the moon and back.

And to John, whom I can't wait to spend the rest
of my life with.

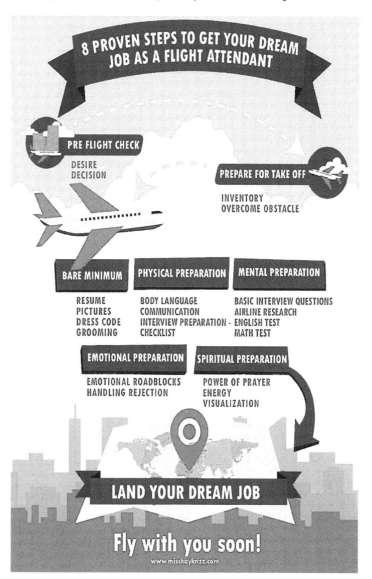

Download your printable PDF Copy of this infographic @ wwww.misskaykrizz.com/blog/freedownload Password: flywithyou

Why can I write a book on
How to become a Flight Attendant?

Maybe some of you are wondering, "Miss Kaykrizz, what gives you the right to write a book about this topic? Aren't these books supposed to be written by people with HR backgrounds? Psychology Majors or even PhDs?"

Sorry, I don't have any of these. I did not even work as a recruiter for my airline. Then, why can I write a book about getting the job as a Flight Attendant?

My most important credentials: my experience in applying and my countless rejections from the airlines that I applied to. Somehow in the ocean of failures, I managed to turn that around and now I'm living my dream life.

Losing Hope

"Should I give up? Or should I keep chasing pavements, even if it might lead me nowhere?"

This is exactly how I felt when I was applying for the position of Flight Attendant for the nth time!

Have you ever been in that situation when the thing that you wanted so so badly was almost within your reach but then it slipped away?

What will you do?

Will you give up?

Or try again?

As a regular girl with no money or connections, I studied hard through countless online searches for related advice and tips. Through research, I grew my confidence on my own and believe me, it was not an easy process.

During those times, I only wished that there was someone who I can look up to whenever I was rejected. That there was someone who knows the technicalities of things whilst applying for the job. That there was someone who knows the secret behind why some get the job and others get the rejection speech.

I badly needed someone who can encourage me to keep on pursuing my dreams of flying no matter what.

But there was no one.

Family was sympathetic, and they were ever supportive. Some friends and colleagues told me maybe it's not meant to be. Most just don't get what it was like. It's not just any application. It was like an *Artista* Search or an audition to enter Pinoy Big Brother's House. It would change your whole life!

Though the love of my family and relatives are there, they couldn't help me when it came to airline technicalities that I'm not familiar with, like low-cost airline or traditional airline and how do they differ, or if you are the cabin crew, where is the best place to work for?

I wrote this book for all of you who want to be a Flight Attendant. Especially for those who have tried and failed. For I have been exactly in the same position.

I am not claiming that I am an expert. I don't have PhD in Psychology. I did not study Psychology nor did I ever work as some HR personnel. I am purely speaking from my own experiences and struggles. What have helped me in my journey of achieving my dream of travelling the world? How did I afford the lifestyle that I have once dreamed of? And how did I have the means to start my own business? All of these I attained by working as a Flight Attendant.

This book is about me chasing the elusive dream job of being a Flight Attendant. Through my multiple rejections and struggles, I have discovered that there are no easy shortcuts, and that no special techniques or magic needed to get the job. All you need is **proper preparation**. Like the famous saying: *Preparation is the key to Success!* If you are ready to get prepping, let's fly right into it.

P.S., As a thank you for buying this book, I have included a lot of free downloads that you can access through my website:

It is written on some parts of the book and you may also refer to them. Please see below:

- 1 Page PDF Summary of the 8 Steps:
  wwww.misskaykrizz.com/blog/freedownload
  Password: flywithyou

- The Flight Attendant Interview Checklist printable PDF:
  http://misskaykrizz.com/blog/interview-preparation-checklist/ *Password: downloadchecklist*
- Sample Resumé PDF:

  http://misskaykrizz.com/blog/sampleresume
  Password: simpleresume

You may also win a FREE Skype Coaching Session with me once you post a photo of you and the book with the hashtag #readyfortakeOff and tag me @misskaykrizz on IG, Twitter and FB. 1 winner will be selected every month and will be announced on my FB Page every end of the month! So make sure to submit your entries!

Fly with you soon!

Miss Kaykrizz

Step One: Preflight Check

Don't Call it a Dream, Call it a Plan

- Anonymous

$\mathcal{D}$o you know what separates an applicant who gets the job and an applicant who gets the *'try again next time'* speech?

90% of the time, successful applicants did what I call a Preflight Check (PFC). From my experience, the results when I applied without doing the PFC and when I did, they are extremely different.

But first, what is Preflight Check?

In aviation, it refers to a routine check that the crew conducts to make sure that all important equipment are present and in good working condition. Failure to do this properly may cause airline accidents. *(Definition from Google and Wikipedia)*

This can make or break the flight, because in case of emergency… out there in the air, there are no stores supplying your immediate needs. You will be stuck with what you have. If Pre-Flight Check was not done correctly, it may cost not only your life but other passengers' lives as well.

Same thing when applying for your dream job. You have to do a proper Preflight Check; otherwise, it may cost you the job opportunity.

So, what are these things that you need to prepare even before writing out your résumé?

They are Desire and Decision.

Let me explain further.

CHAPTER 1

Desire

When the "Why" is clear, the "How" is easy.

- Unknown

Why, in the first place, do you want to become a Flight Attendant?

Is it because you want to have a *selfie* with the Eiffel tower? Do you want to create a photo portfolio and be *instafamous*? Is it because you love exploring new places? Perhaps, do you fancy wearing cute uniforms, walking in high heels and looking as glam as Audrey Hepburn? Or maybe, you just want to prove something to yourself. Maybe you want to escape the current situation that you are in. It could be that you really want to travel and see the world, at the same time taking advantage of the free fare, hotel accommodations and many more to mention. Last but not the least, by working in the service industry, this will let you earn enough money to start your own business after saving for just 2 years, just like me.

Or maybe, you have other reasons I failed to mention. I am not here to judge, as there is no right or wrong reason to be a Flight Attendant.

But there has to be a *reason*.

Being aware of this reason can be the KEY to getting the job. When your WHY is there, depending on how strong is the WHY, believe me you can come up with the HOW and no amount of rejections will to stop you from getting your goal. No matter how corny it may sound to you right now, missing this step is not acceptable. This desire is what makes your eyes sparkle, your smile brighter and your chances of getting hired higher. This is actually how you can create an aura around you that will make you stand out among hundreds of applicants. Don't miss this step, or else you might end up wasting your time. Worse, you might actually get the job but later on realize you didn't really want it.

So, stop reading this book for a moment. Pause and listen to your heart. Find out the real reason why you desire to be a Flight Attendant. List down your top 5 WHYs below or if the space is not enough write it on a piece of paper.

1._____

2._____

3._____

4._____

5._____

CHAPTER 2

Decision

Once you make a decision, the universe conspires to make it happen. - Ralph Waldo Emerson

It all starts with a decision. If you are really decided, no one and no amount of rejection is going to stop you. And in order to make the right decision, first of all, you have to have your facts straight.

Most of us do things because of our own assumptions. More popularly known in the Philippines as "maling akala". So before making your decision, make sure that you know exactly what you are getting yourself into.

I have created a fun Expectations Vs. Reality about being a Flight Attendant. This may not be a complete list, but it does cover the most common ones.

The Flight Attendant Job Description
Google definition:

A Flight Attendant's role is to provide excellent customer service to passengers, while ensuring their comfort and safety throughout the flight.

Expectations:

As a Flight Attendant, everyone would be looking up at you with admiration for your looks, poise or grace. Part of the job is doing those cute demonstrations pointing out the exits, showing how to use those life vests and looking good while doing it.

Reality:

Although it's true that we are mostly good-looking (wink* wink*), we're not just there for the looks. We are primarily there for the safety and comfort of the passengers. Sometimes, we serve passengers their meals and listen to their requests to ensure them a comfortable flight experience. However, we prioritize safety over the service all the time. At times, we have to be assertive and reprimand some passengers who may cause the dissatisfaction of others. That being said, the reality of it and the daily grind of the job is giving service to the customers. We literally serve the passengers, collect their trays and look after their immediate needs. This job requires a person to have an assertive attitude, a humble heart and real passion in customer service.

Expectation:

A Flight attendant eats breakfast in Asia, have lunch in Paris and enjoys dinner in Brazil.

Reality:

Do you want to be a Flight Attendant or a person who can teleport? Just kidding. Having three meals in three different continents within a single day is a very, very difficult task to do considering the travel time, jet lag and the physical fatigue of getting there.

Not all the flights are layovers, layover means you stay in the country that you fly to ranging from 12 hours stay to 3 days max depending on the operations of the airline. There will be flights that you "go and come back" to base on the same day this is what we call a "turn-around" flight. As well as the fact that you may also work on more than one flight for that day. Meaning, you may do 4-6 flights in a single day and still go back home to where you started.

Expectation:

Flight Attendant Training will be as easy as a breeze.

Reality:

Out of a Flight Attendant Training class of thirty (30) students, only around twenty shall graduate the program.

Training is information overload every day. You have to learn the language of aviation, the names of different countries, their respective city's airport codes as well as know how to calculate time differences.

The most important thing is that you will be trained for safety. You will know what to do on all types of emergency scenarios that may possibly happen while on air. You will learn how to do first aid and how to handle hi-jack or bomb threat situations.

Easy breezy? More like hurricane and it's time to take cover!

Flight Attendants....when they find out that training wasn't what they thought it was.

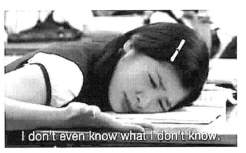

Photo credits to: I Heart Cabin Crew

The Flight Attendant Lifestyle

Expectation:

Being a Flight Attendant, I get to live an easy vacation lifestyle.

Reality:

It's real hard work. Even though we don't have the regular work hours that is 9am-5pm daily, we still put in eight hours or more at irregular times per day.

During holidays and special occasions, we usually miss out on them unless you planned your year ahead of time to be able to get your yearly leaves around these dates.

Also, keeping yourself on tiptop shape should be a priority because of the physical demands of the job. That is why lots of Flight Attendants are into fitness, clean eating, beauty products as well as allocating ample time to sleep during their rest days.

Expectation:

The Flight Attendant job is for the single ladies.

Reality:

We do have married people on the industry, and they can make the schedule work for their families. Most people take maternity leaves and come back to flying after giving birth to their babies.

To summarize, here is the reality of what a Flight Attendant does:

flight at•ten•dant \flit ə-'ten-dənt\ n. Actor; Babysitter; Bartender; Busboy ; Concierge; Conversationalist; Counselor; Dietitian; Dispatcher; Firefighter; Maitre d'; Gourmet Cook; Juggler; Lifeguard; Mind Reader; Mechanic; Model; Negotiator; Nurse; Plumber; Police Officer; Porter; Psychiatrist; Referee; Safety Inspector; Sanitary Engineer; Security Guard; Tour Guide; Travel Consultant; Usher; Valet. But never, never ever use the "S" word!

Photo credits to Pinterest

For the purpose of this book, which is to get the job as a Flight Attendant, it is Important to note the following:

Qualities that the interviewers will be looking for the candidates.

- Team Player
- Responsible
- Has an Understanding Nature
- Confident
- Owns a Good Sense of Humor
- Caring
- Has a Good Grooming

- Motivated
- Enthusiastic
- Dependable
- Friendly
- Resilient
- Patient
- Has a Mature Outlook in life
- Organized
- Effective Listener
- Assertive
- Good Communicator

I hope by now, I have clarified some of the most common misconceptions about the job and lifestyle of Flight Attendants. I also hope that I did not scare you; I wasn't meaning to (just a little bit!).

Having these information, know your own situation, your personality and your lifestyle preference. Armed with these, you can make a better decision if this is the best path for you.

Now, if you have decided to proceed, turn the page and let's get it on!

Step Two:

Prepare for Take Off

Adventure awaits...

- Anonymous

Now we are clear why you want to be a flight attendant and we know exactly what we are getting ourselves into. It's time to begin our preparation.

Where do we start?

CHAPTER 3

Inventory

The door to wisdom is knowing yourself

- Unknown

We have to start from within, of course! Take stock of what you have and see which areas need to be worked on. Just like when you are dressing yourself, you want clothes that compliment your assets. When you are going for an interview, it is the same thing. You are basically selling yourself by highlighting your strengths. How can you do the selling if you yourself don't know what your product is?

In this case, your product is yourself.

Take some time to think and be honest with yourself. List down below what you know about yourself. Having a parent, a friend or significant other help you identify these, is of great help.

Your top 5 strengths

1._____

2._____

3._____

4._____

5._____

Your top 5 weaknesses and what you must do to overcome them.

1._____
2._____
3._____
4._____
5._____

After finishing your list, check out the next part wherein I listed down the things that I believe are non-negotiables for the career of being a Flight Attendant. Check out your own list if you have those qualities on your Strength List. If not, make sure that you work on making them a part of your strength.

CHAPTER 4

Overcome Obstacles

There are many difficult obstacles on your path.
Don't allow yourself to become one of them -
Ralph Marston

I hear a lot of my friends and readers tell me, "I will have LASIK surgery first", or "I will remove my scar / moles first" before they apply. This is a mistake that most people commit. The Flight Attendant's job is so glamorized that people have the misconception that you have to be perfect to be given the opportunity.

The truth is that today's airline industry is not what it was back in the 1950s. Those were the golden days when flying was really a tough industry to get into. Fast forward the 21st century, flying is no longer an occasion that people get dressed for anymore. Most passengers travel in the most comfortable clothes as possible, and airlines have to compete in a very tough market that we see cost cutting everywhere.

For obstacles that may be stopping you to apply for the position, most of them fall under the "90% of the reasons that is not even worth worrying about". However, for the remaining 10% that really matters for airlines nowadays, I have listed it down below:

Airline Non-negotiable List

- Height (Check your height. Each airline has different height requirements.)
- Weight (It should be within the healthy and acceptable BMI relative to your height.)
- English Written and Verbal Skills (Most exams are comprehensive English tests, and English is the language used to communicate during the interview.)
- Confidence (can you speak in public? do you have the right body language)
- Customer Service (Do you know what the words 'customer service' mean?)
- Teamwork (Are you able to work with other people?)
- Medical Fitness (Do you possibly suffer from scoliosis, anemia, vertigo, color blindness, or ear and balance issues?)

I know you may be puzzled why I did not include pimples, scars, teeth, etc. in the list. I purposely did not include those because I truly believe that those are NOT non-negotiables for the airlines industry. Most people get stumped by this. Let me just clarify that you guys don't need to have perfect teeth and flawless skin.

These things are just common misconceptions about the selection process for the Flight Attendant job. Despite having imperfections, the airlines would still hire you depending on the supply and demand of applicants. I have created 2 videos about these topics called

"Can I still be a flight Attendant if _____?"
at *www.youtube.com/misskaykrizz*

You may watch it here:
https://www.youtube.com/watch?v=xKcNswjXB4I
and here
https://www.youtube.com/watch?v=d3iwXF4eRLk

Just bear in mind that if you got the non-negotiables nailed down, all the rest are just useless worrying and things that you can simply find a solution for. Focus on the goal and overcome your own obstacles. Stick to the rule of thumb when applying for an airline.

Meet the Airline Non-negotiable Requirements List

Show up for the interview as prepared as you can be and let your obstacle (i.e. scars, vision, teeth) be dealt with during the medicals. Pass the interview and deal with the tiny details that don't really matter later.

The most important thing is that you gave it a shot.

Chapter 5

Resumé

If opportunity doesn't knock, build a door. - Unknown

Having your resumé or CV (curriculum vitae) prepared is one of the most important Must-Haves for the day of interview. You can forget about wearing your undergarments but you cannot forget to have your resumé with you.

To prepare your resumé, this refers to the physical resumé that you have to print and bring with you on the interview itself. This seems pretty obvious, but some still forget this most basic thing.

1. Make sure that your resumé has your complete and updated contact details. This is where the recruiters will get in touch with you for the second round of assessment.

2. It must be tailor-made for the airline industry. Mention your people skills, the team sports that you have participated in, your customer service experiences, as well as your First Aid training. These are the topics that recruiters will ask you about during your short initial assessment.

3. However, do not make your resumé a 10-page long presentation. Make it as compact as possible with all the important details highlighted.

4. Aside from your resumé, all other documentary requirements must also be carefully packed and brought with you.

   I remember that when Air Asia Philippines was hiring back then, they required everyone to have a resumé, NSO Birth Certificate, NBI clearance, police clearance and 4R Full body and 2x2 headshot pictures. All applicants that have incomplete requirements were not able to enter the premises. So, you have to double check what the airline is requiring its applicants to bring on the day of interview.

5. Keep your resumé in a folder to keep it neat and crisp, but remove the folder when you hand in your resumé to the person in charge.

RESUME

YOUR NAME

Contact Information:
Address: XXXXXX XXXXXXX
Cellphone: XXXXXXX
Email address: xxxxxx@xxxxx.com

Personal Data:
Age: XX Yrs. Old
Sex: Female
Status: Single
Weight: 50 kg
Height: 165 cm.

Educational Background:

College:	2004 - 2009	Bachelor of Science in Nursing University of the XXXX Banilad Campus, Cebu City
High School:	2000 - 2004	St. XXX Educational Center of Leyte Brgy. Abucay, Tacloban City, Leyte
Elementary:	1994 - 2000	XXX Elementary School CAA Compund, Las Piñas City, Metro Manila
Languages: Skills:		Engish, Tagalog &Cebuano Excellent English Communication skills Customer Service Skills Computer and Internet proficient Problem solving and analytical skills

Working and Training Experience:

January 2010 – January 2011	Publishing Consultant (sales) XXXX Corporation Asiatown, IT Park, Lahug, Cebu City 6000
June 2009 – January 2010	Customer Service Representative XXXX Corporation Asiatown, IT Park, Lahug, Cebu City 6000
Aug. 2007- Feb. 2008	Independent Broker International Marketing Group Salinas Drive, Lahug Cebu City
Nov.2006 - Nov. 2007	KFC- Service Crew KFC Store, Cocomall Branch J. Osmeña St. Capitol Site Cebu City, Phillippines

SEMINARS & TRAINING

* University's Student Council Member

* Leadership Training Seminar

* Varsity Swim Team Member

I hereby certify that the above information is true and correct to the best of my knowledge and belief.

YOUR NAME
Applicant

I use a very simple resumé sample, some of you might like to use it, others may want to make it better, but this is what have worked for me.

You may download a PDF Printable version of it here:

http://misskaykrizz.com/blog/sampleresume/

Password: simpleresume

Step Three:

Bare Minimum

Talent will get you in the door, Character will keep you in the room.

- Unknown

The Bare Minimum are the most basic preparations that needed to be done to get yourself past the door. Flight Attendant Recruitments mostly have gate keepers that check your complete requirements before you are allowed to go inside the recruitment area.

CHAPTER 6

Headshot and Full Body Picture

A single picture is worth a thousand words
- Napoleon Bonaparte

For the pictures, it is important that you invest in a good quality photograph. Your photos will be stapled with your resumé, and it will be the first thing that will catch the eye of the recruiter before scanning the rest of your resumé. Most would require a headshot in passport size or 2x2 picture and a full body picture in a business attire, all in light blue background.

Obviously, you have to have these photos taken before the day of the interview. No excessive jewelry, and the hair should be in the proper haircut for men and neatly groomed in a bun or a short hairstyle for women. It would help to have some parts photoshopped but not too much for the recruiters tend to compare it with you during your physical assessment.

Sample of my pictures for Qatar Airways Recruitment:

2x2 Headshot

4R Whole Body Picture

CHAPTER 7

Dress Code

and Grooming

You can have anything you want.
If you dress for it. - Edith Head

The dress code will apply to both your photograph and the interview proper.

Business attire for men will require a formal collared polo shirt, slacks and blazer. Attire must be clean and pressed well.

For footwear, closed leather shoes are preferred, either in black or brown, and wears long socks on the inside. The haircut should be short (1-2 inches from the ear), has no sideburns and the back should not touch the collar. Depending on what airline you are applying for, the hairstyle matters. For conservative airlines (ie.PAL), they abhor anime-like hairstyles. But for fun-loving, adventurous types (i.e. Air Asia), they accept these hairstyles.

Men should have clean and neat nails. No earrings, piercings, bracelets and excessive accessories are allowed. A plain watch will do.

For women, attire will be a formal blouse, skirt and blazer. The hair must be tied neatly in a bun, or if you have a short hairstyle, its backside must not touch the collar. If you are applying for Air Asia, they like their Flight Attendants having their hair styled down and not tied up in a bun. For nails, it would be best to get a manicure in nude, French tip or a classic red color. Minimal accessories are the best to make sure that the attention is focused on you and not your jewelries. A pair of stud earrings, and not dangling earrings, are allowed. An example of a good accessory would be a nice classic watch. Don't wear a necklace and bracelet if possible. Shoes must be closed 2-inch heel shoes. Stockings are not a must. But do shave your legs. Full on make-up with foundation and concealers in place.

I created a video of the 'Things to Bring' on your Flight Attendant interview with examples of the bare minimum items needed for your interview: *https://www.youtube.com/watch?v=mKqCBubBeO4*

Step Four:

Physical Preparation

You will never have a second chance to make a good impression - Will Rogers

At the earlier chapter of this book, I have mentioned about the most commonly asked questions, like: If I have a pimple scar (poor eyesight, a kid, etc., etc., etc.) can I still be a Flight Attendant?

Should you have more doubts, I recommend you to reread 'Chapter 4: Overcoming Obstacles'. This time, I will not talk about things like make-up, shoes and clothes. These, I already discussed on the previous chapter.

Here I would like to focus on your physical body. On how you can exude the most confidence on the way you present yourself, verbally and nonverbally during your interview.

CHAPTER 8

Body language

Your body communicates as well as your mouth.
Don't contradict yourself. - Allen Ruddock

We have all heard of the quote: "Action Speaks Louder than Words", and I say that this is especially true when it comes to Flight Attendant job interviews. In fact, I believe that 80% of what the interviewers assess are based on the non-verbal cues like how the candidates express themselves, how they look as well as how they behave. Knowing this, you need to make sure that in front of the recruitment staff, you must be aware of these cues.

If you have seen my tips videos, you may have noticed my mantra: 1. Establish eye contact 2. Be aware of your posture and 3. Smile. I say this to all my videos as mantra so you can easily remember it. For me, this is very effective because when I am nervous I tend to forget everything. This mantra keeps me focused and composed even if my hands are literally shaking. Eye contact, posture, smile. Eye contact, posture, smile. Eye contact, posture, smile. This can really save your life.

Eye Contact

Establishing eye contact is the most basic means of communication. It's the way to connect to the interviewer. Intense and prolonged eye contact is not necessary, but a healthy dose of it is required. Doing eye contact shows that you are confident and trustworthy. Eye contact affects a person's perception of another so make sure that you use it to your advantage. If you are not comfortable holding eye contact while speaking to the person, you may look around the person's eyes, forming an imaginary triangle. Rotating your focus on this triangle will give the illusion that you are giving eye contact without forcing it.

Posture

Always be aware of posture because this can mean everything. Slouching gives the impression that you are either tired or unconfident. Tensed shoulders show that you are nervous. Fidgeting means you can't handle stress and can't keep yourself calm under pressure.

When sitting down, sit upright and at the edge of the chair. Hands on your lap and put your legs together. When standing, chest out — stomach in and chin up. Act as if a string is pulling you from the top of your head, and drop your shoulders. A more visual tutorial can be found on my video here:

https://www.youtube.com/watch?v=w-Mk_XXwhNY

Smile

A good smile is a requirement. Not only is this applicable on your photos or during the introductions, but also all throughout the assessment day. A smile that is sincere and represents warmth is what you need. It is understandable that you will not be smiling for no reason at all, so look for a chance to show off that smile. One of these opportunities is when you happen to have an eye contact for the first time, to the recruiter or your co-applicant. I also almost always hear this quote from veteran applicants: "Smile like it's the happiest day of your life! Like it is your wedding day". I know for sure this truly helped me with my applications.

When you are focused and are mindful of these three traits throughout the interview day, you have will have a great aura about you that the recruiter would surely notice. You will stand out among the rest. Once again the mantra is: Eye Contact, Posture, and Smile.

CHAPTER 9

Communication

Communication works for those who work on it
- John Powell

Communication is a two-way process. It involves the ability to express yourself and your ability to listen.

Being able to express yourself in straight English is an advantage. To improve your English skills, an old school trick that I do to improve is practice reading the newspaper out loud every morning. If you find a word that you don't understand, look it up and learn how to pronounce it.

When it comes to listening, there are two forms — verbal and non-verbal. Verbal listening skills are those acknowledgement expressions that you say in order to let the other person know that you agree or disagree to what they are saying. examples of these are phrases like 'I understand what you are saying", "Yes, I agree", and "I am sorry to hear that".

Non-verbal listening skills involves body language and facial expression. Being in an open stance, nodding when you are in agreement, smiling, frowning and laughing at the right moment are all examples of non-verbal communication.

During the assessment, keep in mind that the moment you enter the room, you are being assessed non-stop of these skills. Both the verbal and nonverbal communication skills. Make sure that you demonstrate them effectively all throughout the process.

I highly suggest that you practice these skills before the day of the assessment for you to exude sincerity and avoid appearing fake in your actions.

CHAPTER 10

The Flight Attendant

Interview Checklist

Don't expect success, Prepare for it. - Unknown

Bare Minimum Checklist	
Resumé	
Picture (4R Full Body and 2x2 Headshot)	
Business Attire prepared	
Other specific airline requirements (NBI, Birth Certificate, etc.)	
Check Height (Consistent with airline requirement)	
*BMI (Body Mass Index - Consistent with airline requirement if required)	
Physical Appearance Checklist - Male	
Hair (clean cut and formally styled, no wild colors - roots not showing)	

Facial Hair (clean shave)	
Nails (clean and groomed)	
Tattoos (keep hidden)	
Tie (choose one that reflects your personality)	
Suit (Use a professional looking suit, keep it creaseless, take it off on your commute / drive on the way to the interview venue)	
Shoes (clean and polished)	
Accessories (no flashy items, a wristwatch will do. Remove any piercings)	
Physical Appearance Checklist - Female	
Hair - (Bun make sure no strands are sticking out or styled if shorter than the collar of your blouse, no wild hair colors - roots not showing)	
Full Make-up (cover any imperfections)	
Nails (well-groomed and polished with red, nude or French tip)	
Accessories (no flashy items, a wristwatch and stud earrings will do)	

Suit (Use a professional looking suit dress or blouse and skirt combo, keep it creaseless, take it off on your commute / drive on the way to the interview venue)	
Shoes (clean and polished)	
Mental Prep Checklist (see chapter 5)	
Answers to basic questions prepared, memorized and practiced spontaneous delivery	
Airline Company Researched (tagline, CEO, destinations, etc.)	
Role of the Flight attendant fully understood and researched.	
Guaranteed Success Checklist	
Get enough sleep before the interview day	
Eat healthy food (you are what you eat)	
Interview venue and time are confirmed	
Plan on how to get to the interview on time complete	

Motivated and Enthusiastic Attitude worked on	
Effective Communication Skills practiced (speaking and listening)	
Emotional Roadblocks have been identified and settled (to be discussed more in Chapter 6)	
Spiritual Preparation done	

Table 1.1 Interview Preparation Checklist created by Miss Kaykrizz

Download The Flight Attendant Interview Checklist printable PDF: *http://misskaykrizz.com/blog/interview-preparation-checklist/ Password: downloadchecklist*

Step Five:

Mental Preparation

Until you're mentally ready, you will never be physically prepared. - Ish Shh

How many times has it happened that your mind goes blank when put in the spotlight?

To avoid these occurrences, it is important to prepare yourself mentally for the day of the interview.

CHAPTER 11

Basic Interview Questions

A job interview is not a test of your knowledge, but your ability to use it at the right time. - Anonymous

These are the questions that I guarantee 100% the interviewer will ask, unless you are their 2000th candidate for that day — they'd probably throw wild questions just to ease their boredom. A tip is, if you can, make sure to be the first one in the interview queue. That way you can face the interviewers at their optimum state rather than at the end of the day where all they'll want is to finish everything and leave.

Now get a piece of paper, and write down your own answers to these questions. Memorize it and practice delivering it in a non-robotic, spontaneous manner.

Top tip: Practice delivering your answers out loud in front of a mirror, and later on in front of your family or friends.

Tell me about yourself.

This is the favorite 'Ice Breaker' during the interview. It is important to have a prepared answer for this question. It is the opportunity for you to sell yourself and show them how knowledgeable you are about the position you are applying for. And, how to do just that?

Don't make the mistake of talking about your family background, relationship status or your pets and any other really personal but unrelated information. What this question is asking about are your professional **experiences** and trainings will help **qualify** you for the position, **outside interests** to see what kind of person you are and your **ambition** for them to see how far will you go on your career.

Therefore, it is safe to talk about your educational background, the seminars you attended or extracurricular activities that you have gone through. Mention how that is related to the position that you are applying for.

It is also key to note that you have to keep your answer as brief as possible so as to not be tagged as a person that "can't stop talking about himself". Keep your answers to 1 - 2 minutes' tops.

First step, of course, is to know what are the qualities required of a Flight Attendant. This would allow you to fully understand what the job is. Refer to Chapter 1.

But, what if you are a fresh graduate and have NO work experience at all? You can still sell yourself by showing that you did your research about the position and that you have the qualifications as good as anyone else. For example, you may mention that you were part of the swimming team while at school (swimming being part of the Flight Attendant Training, thus it is relevant). You may also mention any instance where you've been part of an organization, the school student government or varsity team (Teamwork is very important as a cabin crew member). If you have any experience with Customer Service, like having a part-time job while in school, that would be a plus (customer Service is one big aspect of the career of being a flight attendant).

I created a fun video on how to answer this question, including a sample answer. You may check it out @ *youtube.com/misskaykrizz*

What is your edge among other candidates?

Basically, this is the same question as *Tell Me About Yourself* but it is *umpped* up to the next level. So your answer should be as well.

People will answer this question in different ways, but the way I do it (and I find very effective) is to structure my response around qualities that are most relevant to the position. I tell a short true story about my life wherein I demonstrated those qualities.

Here are the key qualities:

Motivated

Assertive

Trustworthy

Responsible

Team player

Patient

Enthusiastic

Reliable

Organized

Dedicated

Committed

Has Positive Attitude

Has Strong Work Ethic

Sample Answer:

(use sample as reference and write your own version on your paper. It is important the you state facts and also it is easier to remember)

"My edge among other candidates is my Positive Attitude. I have been through many struggles in my career, and at times when the going is really tough, I manage to get through them with the right mindset. An example of this is on my previous work in a call center company. While everyone was struggling with the swing night shifts, and my teammates were all cranky because we were sleepy, I got through it by not engaging on negative talks about the schedule, and getting enough sleep in the morning and in between breaks. I would initiate funny stories with my team that eventually helped my team go through that grueling week and achieve our team's targets. I think all of us here are qualified for the job but my commitment to always stay positive really is my edge."

What are your strengths?

It is best to focus on work-related strengths when answering this question. Take 3 key qualities that you have and cite an example where you demonstrated them.

Sample Answer:

(use sample as reference and write your own version on your paper. It is important the you state facts and also it is easier to remember)

"I can say that I have a passion for customer service. While working as a Customer Service Agent on my previous job, I was consistent on keeping my satisfaction ratings on top. I also find personal satisfaction when I am genuinely able to help people solve their problems."

The thing here is that anyone can say that his or her strengths are this and that, but giving concrete examples and success stories from your own experience gives you more credibility and gets you a higher score on the interview ratings.

What are your weaknesses?

The biggest mistake you can make when answering this question is saying that you don't have a weakness.

Acknowledging one's shortcomings is a strength itself, so you must have at least 2 ready answers for this question.

However, make sure that you describe your weakness in a positive light so that you won't hurt your application.

Sample Answer:

(use sample as reference and write your own version on your paper. It is important the you state facts and also it is easier to remember)

"I have a tendency to be a perfectionist in everything that I do, so sometimes the tasks that were assigned to me would take more time for me to do than the usual. I am so fascinated by details that sometimes it gets in the way of my efficiency. After getting a feedback from my team leader on this matter, it had a positive effect on me. I have been able to apply it to my work and find a balance between efficiency and details of doing my job."

Giving answers like this is like slashing with a double-edged sword. You answered the question, and at the same time, you also demonstrated other positive qualities (i.e. accepting constructive criticism, being able to look at yourself and change when needed) which ultimately are strengths.

Where do you see yourself 5 years from now?

One of the most common questions and highly likely will be asked of you. The right amount of confidence (meaning, avoid being arrogant) and positivity will be your best bet.

Wrong answers are: "I don't know", "no one can really predict the future right?" or "I want to be at the same position that you (the interviewer) are now". (Too arrogant!)

A good answer will include you being still employed in the company and having progress both professionally and personally.

Sample Answer:

(use sample as reference and write your own version on your paper. It is important the you state facts and also it is easier to remember)

"I see myself as a perfect fit for this job. If given the opportunity, I would like to further my skills and understanding of my role and the company culture. Later on, I want to establish myself as one of the best cabin crews in my field.

Also, I would like to improve my educational requirements by taking a part-time or online course that would help me build myself as a qualified candidate on any advanced position that may open in the company."

CHAPTER 12

Airline Specific Research

Be so good that they can't ignore you. -
Anonymous

*M*ake sure that you put in the work to research about these airline facts. This shows that you are not just applying for any airline openings but you are being professional and are interested with this specific airline that you are applying for. And that alone can get you the job offer.

Now here are the interview questions asked specifically for Flight Attendant applicants, and how to tackle them. As you have done with the previous exercise:

- Get a piece of paper.

- Write down your personal answers.

- Memorize it.

- Practice delivering the answers spontaneously in front of the mirror.

- Practice in front of family and friend's / support system.

Research Checklist:

For these questions, each and every airline will have a different 'right' and 'preferred' answer, so you have to answer these questions depending on their preference.

- What is the airline's tagline?
- How many and what are the airline's destinations?
- Does the airline have expansion or growth plans?
- What is the history of this airline?
- Where are the airline's hub locations?
- Who are the airline's competition?
- How long has the airline been in operation?
- What products and services do they offer? Do they have a frequent flyer program? What is the name of that program?
- What do you like about this airline?
- Who is the airline's CEO and key people?
- What does the airline's brand represent?

Now, let us tackle the questions that you will ONLY see in a Flight Attendant interview. I have included what to focus on while answering them as well as a sample answer.

Why do you want to be a cabin crew?

Focus on:

- the main reason for wanting to become a flight attendant (your ambition)
- your suitability for the role
- positive aspects of the job.
- working in the service industry.

Sample Answer:

(*use sample as reference and write your own version on your paper. It is important the you state facts and also it is easier to remember*)

"I have always wanted to become a Flight Attendant ever since my first flight as a kid. My experience gave me such a pleasant memory that from then on, I have aspired to become a member of the flight attendant team.

Even though I very much enjoy my current job, I aspire now to have a career that is hands-on, challenging, varied and exciting.

I firmly believe that my attributes and qualities suit the role of a Flight Attendant. I enjoy working with a team where everyone is trying to achieve the same goal.

I understand that delivering high level customer service is the bread and butter of this industry, and this is something that I enjoy in a career."

Side note: Notice that I did not mention any cliché answers when tackling this question such as, "I want to travel the world for free", "I think I have the looks and personality of a flight attendant", "It has been my dream to fly", and "I want to have free tickets for me and my family". Even though this may all be true, you have to understand that employment is a business transaction. It has to be a win-win situation for both parties. If you only focus on your win and failed to mention the company's win if they hire you, you give the impression that this is going to be a one-sided relationship. Thus, key takeaway, mention that you want this and why you would be suitable for it.

Why do you want to join our airline?

Focus on:

- the airline's reputation (make sure it is a positive one)
- that you are not just applying for any airline but you are interested in this specific airline by showing that you have researched about them

- the quality of the airline's product and services
- what the airline's brand stands for

Sample Answer:

(use sample as reference and write your own version on your paper. It is important the you state facts and also it is easier to remember)

"Before applying to your airline, I have researched several other airline companies and end up deciding to apply here. I like that you have superior customer service, and I know that your company have a great reputation.

I have also spoken with some of your employees, and I am very happy to report that they are very happy with their career. They said that you are an excellent employer. I like the fact that your airline is always looking for ways to improve and innovate.

I like to work with an airline that listens to its customers, which I see you practice. I know that a good airline that always strive to give its passengers positive and pleasant experiences will be here to stay for a long time. And, I would love to be a part of that kind of airline.

I believe that I have the qualities to be a great part of this team. Given the chance, I wish to help this company keep itself ahead of its competition."

What happened with your previous application with our airline? (if this is a repeat application)

Focus on:

- the positive (never give a frown or a vibe of sadness)
- the learnings you have found out about yourself and the airline industry.
- how ready you are for the opportunity this time around

Sample Answer:

(use sample as reference and write your own version on your paper. It is important the you state facts and also it is easier to remember)

"My previous application was such a positive experience for me, even though I did not get the job at that time. I have learned so much about myself and the airline industry. It had heightened my curiosity and moved me to research more about flying and the role of a Flight Attendant. I found out that there are more to being a Flight Attendant than what meets the eye. I made friends and contacts with people that I have applied with and it was great. Today, I made sure that I am well prepared and ready to take on the role of a Flight Attendant. I want to prove to you that I am a suitable candidate and a perfect fit for the job."

What challenges do you see our airline will face in the future, and how can you, as the flight attendant, help overcome those challenges?

Purpose of this question:

- To assess your knowledge about the airline industry

The airline industry is a very competitive industry. It faces a lot of challenges when it comes to cost of operations and security issues. At the same time, it is expected to deliver a very high level of service keeping up with the expectations of passengers.

- To assess your knowledge about your role as a Flight Attendant.
  - The Flight Attendant is the face of the airline. It can be compared to the first line of firing squad if you compare it to battle. The role of the Flight Attendant covers a big part of the whole passenger experience, that is why no matter what the airline is, traditional or budget, it is a must for the Flight

Attendant to always deliver superior customer service. This means that you must be friendly, be all-smiles and be willing to always assist and listen to the customers.

Focus on:

– your awareness of the industry issues (like competition, security and high operating cost)
– the customer's idea of what an airline should be and manage their expectations effectively, even exceed it if possible
– your understanding of the role of a Flight Attendant in delivering crucial service to the customer and that if you do well, customers are most likely to come back

Sample Answer:

(use sample as reference and write your own version on your paper. It is important the you state facts and also it is easier to remember)

"I can see that in the airline business, the biggest challenge is the competition among others in the industry. Everyone wants to prove they are the best, and the customers in turn wants to pay less for more services.

In addition to this, I see that security issues and financial implications affect the airline industry. This means more security training and procedures are needed, which in turn, results to salary expenses on top of the operating cost and fuel increase cost. This may push the price of airline tickets to increase as well.

Therefore, it is imperative that the Flight Attendant provides the best customer service at all times. It is a known fact that people are willing to pay a little bit extra for excellent service, and the flight attendants are the ones that make it happen.

Making sure that the customer is happy would benefit the airline very much. Not only will they become a loyal customer, but also, they will recommend us to their families and friends.

www.misskaykrizz.com

CHAPTER 13

Push yourself, because no one else is going to do it for you. - Anonymous

Aside from the face-to-face interview, most airlines conduct an English exam for its candidates. This measures the person's communication skills which is important since you will be working with different people from different countries.

The most common English Tests would consist of:

- Reading and Comprehension
- Grammar
- Vocabulary and Spelling

There are a lot of free online tests that you can practice on. Here are a few of them:

https://www.easyenglish.com/

https://www.ego4u.com/en/cram-up/tests/london-dungeon

https://www.ego4u.com/en/cram-up/vocabulary

http://www.examenglish.com/KET/KET_grammar.htm

https://www.testprepreview.com/modules/reading1.htm

If this is an area that you need to work on, please invest some time on it. Most airlines have a standard passing score, and if you don't reach it, your application will not be pursued.

CHAPTER 14

Math Test

Don't stress. Do your best. Forget the rest.

- Unknown

You may think that because you will be flying around the world, math has nothing to do with it at all. You may be dismayed because some math is important for practical reasons, as well as for passing the interview.

Algebra, fractions and calculus, of course, will not be asked from you. However, calculating Time Zones will be part of the test and will be very handy even after you start flying.

Some samples of math word problems will look like this:

The departure time of John's plane is at 4pm local time. Ruth lives 17 hours behind John. What time did the plane depart with Ruth's local time?

Answer:

What is 17 hours before 4pm? 11pm

Valuable resources on how to learn manually calculating time zones and flight times math problems:

https://www.slideshare.net/eovelasco/tou-37674228

Step Six:

Emotional

Preparation

We repeat what we don't repair. - Christine Langley- Baugh

Even if you prepare your bare minimums, physical and mental preparations or even if you ultimately get the job of your dreams, if your emotions are not in check, it can ultimately become your undoing.

Let me tell you a story of a Pinay Flight Attendant who got the job with me. After going through the 3-day assessment interviews, the 4-month wait to get a reply, the medicals worth P2,500, the wait for the visa to arrive, the P55,000 agency's placement fee, and the move from the Philippines to the Middle East, she realized that she is ultimately not prepared for her dream.

You may be wondering, "What happened?"

After just a month of training, she was not able to take it anymore. She misses her daughter so badly, she got home-sickness. She started developing a heart condition, and she became really ill. Then, she had to terminate her contract with the company, go home to the Philippines after paying the P55,000 non-refundable placement fee for our agency. I'm not sure if she paid the 2-year training bond (where we could not quit ahead of time, or else we have to pay the fee). That bond is more than $2,000.00 or more than P90,000.00 in cash, give or take a few.

When she got home, she was reunited with her daughter, and I believe her health condition improved.

Our body and emotions are connected; no matter whether we like it or not. Thus, it only makes sense to make sure that you check this aspect of yourself. To save you and your family a lot of money, hassle and adjustments, be honest and really look within yourself.

CHAPTER 15

Emotional Roadblocks

Obstacles are those frightful things that you see
when you take your eyes off your goal.

- Henry Ford

Some questions that you may have to consider are:

Is this what I really want?

- Is this something that you, in your hearts of hearts, want to pursue and happen in your life?
- Is it something that your parents want you to pursue?
- Is it something that you just want to try because you saw some of your friends in social media posting how great their jobs are?

Of course, I will be happy once I achieve my dream job. However, how will I adjust to my new life?

- Will I be okay away from my family and friends?
- Did I mentally and emotionally prepared myself from getting out of my comfort zone?

And this one is a biggie.

- How about my boyfriend/ girlfriend?
- Will he / she stay faithful?
- Will we break-up?
- Am I ready for that, in case that happens?

If these emotions have not been checked and dealt with, they can haunt you while you are on your interview. causes you to say the wrong words, have a mental block, become too nervous that you can't form sentences and be not on the top of your game.

Take your time in answering these questions and give your mind some allowance to adjust to the idea. When the time comes that you get that golden call, there is no turning back.

Success comes to those who are fully prepared. That just doesn't mean your resumé, make-up and interview questions. It also means getting emotionally prepared for a life-changing career.

CHAPTER 16

Handling Rejection

Rejection is neither an indication of value or talent. If you believe in what you offer, then don't stop offering it simply because some some of those you offer it to reject it. Many people are simply not good at recognizing talent or value. It doesn't mean you won't eventually find an audience that will. -Zero Dean

I remember back when I was still a Flight Attendant in Cebu, I dreamed of flying international. I would wake up very early to catch the 4am flight together with my applying buddies. We would fly to Manila to attend the Open Day (initial interview day). We would go straight from the airport to where the event was held. We would line up for 2-3 hours to wait for our turn. We would finish the interview, have lunch and wait until 7-8pm. If we did not get a text message that we are invited for the second day, we would head to the airport and take the last flight going back to Cebu. It was an 11pm flight, meaning we would arrive by midnight.

The next day, we might have a 5am flight, and we have to be ready in order to keep our jobs. It was a sad day if you don't get invited to at least the next round of interviews. My friend and I would be depressed. I remember one time she was expressing her sorrow to me. She said "Kaykrizz, I am so tired of this. Maybe it's just not meant to be? Maybe it's just not for me."

I would tell her that of course that's not true, that maybe it's just not yet the right time for us.

And I would be laughing a few weeks later because that same friend called me up and informed me of another hiring event happening soon! She was so excited and would say "Ruth, there is another hiring! Naka-hearing ko! (I heard of the super-secret news) This is it pancit! Let's go!!!"

She would be so enthusiastic that you will not think that this is the same friend that was depressed and ready to give up just a week ago.

To tell you the truth, it really worked for her. In fact, she was hired internationally before I even did. She was almost 1 year ahead of me. And I am so proud of her. She became the inspiration for all of us back in Cebu. Everyone looked at her and her tenacity. We all know how many times she had applied and failed, and finally she got it. It was a celebration.

"Pain is inevitable, suffering is optional."

-famous Buddhist quote

Let's face it, rejections are painful. However, if we go on living our lives trying to avoid rejection, we will not live a full life at all, let alone have a chance to make our dreams come true. Handling rejection is a life skill, and once you master it, you will do so much better at life.

Some tips on how to handle rejection:

1. Accept what happened, and deal with the pain. The more you deny it (for example: rationalizing: 'oh, I really don't want to get that job anyway', defensiveness: 'on second thought, I don't want to work for that company') the more you will not learn from the experience. Let yourself feel the pain, and let it go through your body. Say to the pain, "I see you and I am here for you". The pain will go away on its own and you'll feel that you've become a stronger person. The more you resist it, the more it will persist. The memory of the pain may become a trigger to your future applications, causing you to experience mental blocks, or to say the wrong words.

So, better deal with it now than to have it haunt you forever.

2. Timing. Know that the timing plays a big part. Sometimes, life just flows on its own timing. A rejection is not a no forever. It just means 'not yet', and it's up to you whether you should keep on asking for what you want in life, or to cave in and settle. Sometimes, a rejection from a company may be a blessing in disguise. You just don't see it yet right now, but in the future when you look back in your life, you may understand why.

3. Taking the rejection too personally is not a good idea. Sometimes, a rejection has totally nothing to do with you as a person. Sometimes, the rejection is not about you. There's a possibility that the company may have exceeded their quota, or their aircraft order got cancelled.

4. Focus on what you can control, and let go of the things you can't control. Focus on areas like your resumé, your grooming, and your research. If ever you still got rejected after that, know that their decision is beyond your control. What is within the limit of your control is on whether you will review your performance and improve your skills, or will

you sulk and choose to be depressed for a long time and swear off being a flight attendant?

5. Think of a rejection as a numbers game. I've always told my brother back when he was call center job that to apply for ten companies before you will get hired. Because of that, my brother did not lose hope even after his 5th interview rejection. Instead, he became more motivated to get the no's out of the way, because by the law of numbers, it is guaranteed that, he will get a job after his 10th attempt. Given that he learned something from each application and improved his style for the next one.

Step Seven:

Spiritual Preparation

Spirituality doesn't come from religion. It comes from our soul.
- Anthony Douglas Williams on his book:
Inside the Divine Pattern

Humans are 'mind, body and soul' beings. In the Catholic teaching, this is the equivalent of the Holy Trinity. I don't mean to preach on this chapter, but I just want to recognize the existence of a higher power at work in this universe.

When I speak of spiritual preparation, it means more than just having the belief that praying to God will help you achieve your dreams. You may say, "Yes, I am confident I am worthy I can do it. I will ask God, and he will give it to me if it's meant to be". Merely saying these things without basis, without the deep understanding of how the world works, will not make sense. They will seem like empty mantras that you keep repeating, and you'll wonder why they are not effective.

I can't say that what I am about to write is the absolute truth. I would just like to share with you the belief that I have and how it helped me achieve my dreams.

The reason I have confidence is because of this bible verse: "I can do all things through Christ which strengthens me". I believe in it with all of my heart and soul.

Being born a Catholic and schooled in Catholic schools my whole academic life, the Catholic teaching became a big part of who I am. Even though I grew up in a less-than-ideal household, I have Jesus, and I hold close to my heart the abovementioned passage. My faith has helped me go through the most difficult times in my life.

As I grew older, I have come to terms with awakening, meaning that I questioned everything including my religion. I then started studying successful people, how they achieved their dreams, and where their confidence come from. It led me to become aware of the new age way of thinking, like the law of attraction, their individual philosophies and beliefs, and the 'what's' that made them successful. Strangely enough, it led me to study life before my Catholic religion has ever been established. I studied the history of ancient Egyptians, Buddhism beliefs, Indian Maharajas, Chinese empires, Muslim Teachings and many more. This kind of search surprisingly did not discourage me from my faith. Rather, it gave me a deeper understanding of the teachings of the Bible. I realized how universal the bible teachings are and how every religion in the world or influential being is trying to teach mankind the same thing.

A big thanks to people like Bo Sanchez, I was able to see a great example of how staying true to your Catholic beliefs. Adopting to ideas like 'abundance being rich' and 'abundant in all aspects of your life' are not just with money but in everything. I was able to see that it is possible to have my Catholic faith stay strong and at the same time, understand how the world works.

In a nutshell, Science and Quantum Physics, modern religion, and ancient civilizations, they tell the same story. There is this one big source (called god, energy and many other names), and we are made from this source (Science call it the Big Bang Theory, and Catholics says that we are all made from the image and likeness of God. Therefore, it also means that we are God, we are energy, we are one with the One. Because of this, we have the power to create the universe. Philosophers quoted, 'Heaven or hell is painting that we paint and we live on it now', while the Catholic teachings say, 'Ask and you shall receive'. New age believers call this the law of attraction.

Having this understanding got me the confidence and the courage to pursue my dreams, in spite of all the doubts and fears I have inside me.

Now, I know that my belief may raise some eyebrows among people. However, I do not want you to accept this reality if it is simply not yours. I don't want to force you or anything. I don't want to prove that I am right and your belief is wrong. I just know that having a profound belief of who you are and your worth, and having basic understanding of how our world works, will lead you to live the dream life that you are dreaming of.

CHAPTER 17

The Power of Prayer

Prayer is when you talk to God. Meditation is when you listen to God. - Unknown

For religious people, this is a no brainer. Offering a prayer to God for your intentions and taking the actions to achieve them is not a difficult concept to believe.

Bible Verses:

"Ask, it shall be given unto you. Seek and you shall find. Knock, the doors will be opened." Mark 7:7

"Therefore I tell you, whatever you ask for in prayer, believe that you have received it, and it will be yours." Mark: 11:24

For those non-Catholics, or would consider themselves atheists, scientologist, new age etc., here is what I can tell you.

If you follow on the lives of successful people like Steve Jobs, Bill Gates, Henry Ford and even Sofia from #girlboss, you would notice that things were not handed down to them. For every self-made man or woman, you will notice a common theme. They all intended to be successful. They have a strong desire in their hearts, and every day they would do something toward achieving that desire until it is finally fulfilled. You may notice that they employed a lot of different techniques such as meditation, visualization and affirmation. They would also emphasize words like focus, determination, gratitude, resilience, and belief in themselves that they can do it.

Successful people don't go through their lives seeing where the tide will take them, hoping that success comes their way. They take charge. They pause and review their intentions and think about that every single day. If you ask me, it's the same practice that we do when we pray. When we pray we ask God, and we believe God has already given it to us. If you study the law of attraction, it is basically the same thing except that you are asking the universe / the major energy source where we all came from and believe and act as if it is already given to you. The simple act of focusing on what you want and producing the feelings of as if you already gained it will perform miracles in your life.

CHAPTER 18

Energy

Your energy introduces you, even before you speak. - Anonymous

Have you ever heard of the phrases, "I like that girl, magka-vibes kami (we have the same vibes)!" or "This place has such nice vibes! That song gives me great vibes!"

This vibe is what I refer to as energy. We all know it exist, and now I want to share with you how you can prepare the vibe for your Flight Attendant Interview!

First, understand that energy or vibe is contagious. Have you ever heard of a comment, 'Negative people are such downers and have such a bad vibe about them'? Have you ever been in a networking event where the people seem to be rallying, enthusiastic about what they are offering? It's a sales strategy, and even Apple uses it to their advantage. So should you.

Second, aim for having a high vibration. You've got to be in this high vibration state in order to give off this vibe to the people that you meet.

Third, raise your energy vibration. How?

Law of Gratitude

This means be grateful for what you already have. The law states that if you are already grateful for what you have, more blessings will come your way. This is what we call in Filipino "siksik liglig". That's the kind of blessings that will come to you if you apply the law of gratitude in your life. It is simple, and you can start as early as now. List down 3 things that you are grateful for in the morning and at night. When you do this, don't just randomly list, "I'm grateful I'm alive", "I have a house", etc. When you write the things that you are grateful for, make sure that you write it with feelings. You must really feel in your heart that you are grateful for such things that is present in your life.

Listen to inspiring music

I love listening to music of my favorite Flight Attendant movies as well as anything related to flying. I literally made a Flight Attendant interview day playlist. I would listen to this music while waiting in line for my turn for the interview. You know those lines that takes 1-2 hours? The playlist is also useful on the commute on the way to the interview. Even on the morning of the interview, I had music playing on loudspeaker while I did my make-up.

What this does is to put me in a really good mood. Music sends really nice chills up and down my spine. The kind of like telling me, 'You got this!', "You're flying already!" and "Claim it!" Hehehehe

Sample music I have on my playlist:

♪ No sign of any rain ♫

♪ I believe I can fly ♫

♪ Rocketeer - Far East Movement ♫

♪ International Smile - Katie Perry ♫

♪ Defying gravity ♫

You can totally make your own list, what I have here are just some of the songs that motivates me and puts me in a great vibe.

CHAPTER 19

Visualization

If you can imagine it and visualize it, you can create it. - The Secret, Law of attraction.

As you are listening to your playlist, visualize yourself already a Flight Attendant, walking on the airport and lugging your trolley behind you, smiling from ear to ear and walking with a beat in every step.

This is very effective coupled with the feelings of happiness, joy or gratitude.

To take your visualization to the next level is to visualize how exactly your interview is going to be like, what questions are going to be ask of you? visualize yourself answering the questions with flying colors. This technique is widely used by athletes before their sports events. The athlete would be instructed by their coach to visualize his or her play, vividly imagining every detail. Then, they would instruct the athletes to visualize themselves doing the play successfully. When this technique was researched, the athlete is connected to a machine that measures brain activity and muscle activity.

Researchers found out that while the athletes are visualizing their play on their minds, the same muscles are activated even though they are not performing at that time. The research further concludes that, the percentage of athletes earning gold medals is positively correlated with practice visualization.

In short, if you have been there in the mind, you will be there in the body. Your body doesn't know the difference whether the event is happening in reality or just in your mind. By practicing the event and success in your mind, you are helping your body get there in reality.

Step Eight:

Take Action to Land

Your Dream Job

What do you call the distance between your dream and your reality? Action. - Anonymous

My take-away for you is that I want you to know that applying for your dream job doesn't have to be trial-and-error or a mystery that you just can't solve. I have already gone through that, and because of that, you don't have to.

I hope you learn from my experience and not make the same mistakes I made. (If you total all my rejections from airline recruitment days, it would be around 20 ++)

The point that I hope to make in this book is: Should you be successful in preparing for the opportunity, I am 100% sure that you will be able to get the job of your dreams.

It's not an easy way to do it, but it sure is worth a try.

You see, the easy way to go is to 'wing it". In the Philippines, it's called the 'Bahala Na' attitude. I want to encourage you through this book to become proactive in trying to achieve your dream.

Yes, you can't control how many people will show up on the recruitment day. You also cannot control how the interviewers will react to your resumé, your interview answers and your looks.

But this, I can tell you for sure. You have the FULL control on how you are going to show up on that recruitment day. Will you show up confident, composed and fully prepared, mind, body and soul? Or, will you show up there and be a nervous wreck, unprepared and leaving everything to faith?

The choice is up to you.

CHAPTER 20

Action Steps

You don't have to be great to get started. You have to get started to be great. - Les Brown

I would like to leave you with a call to action on this last step. I made it purposely a step because this whole system will not work without the last step.

And that is to take ACTION.

You can read every book on how to get this job, but in the end still not get anywhere if you don't take action. Action is the key to success! Now, if there are no openings yet as of the time you are reading this book, it is the perfect opportunity for you to start your preparation. Like I said in the introduction of this book, preparation is the key to success.

To summarize this book, here are the Actions Steps that you can take to kick start your preparation.

Review your answers on Chapter 1. Once and for all, be specific, honest and clear, why do you want to become a Flight Attendant?

1. Decide to pursue the job application despite any obstacles you have in mind. Check that you meet the Airline Non-Negotiable List on Chapter 2.

2. Complete your answers to possible interview questions. Write them down, memorize and practice delivering the answer in front of the mirror. Practice your facial expression, and smile during pauses. (This is the meat of your preparation. Like your guns and bullet when you are going to battle. Don't leave the house without it!)

3. Create your Flight Attendant Interview Song playlist on your phone.

4. Subscribe to my Hiring Alerts Email List, where you would be informed of the airlines hiring and their respective schedules (Philippines only). The earlier you know that there will be an open day (Hiring Event), the better for your preparation. *Subscribe to the Free Hiring Alert Emails*

5. If you are struggling with issues not mentioned in this book, you may hire me for a Skype Session for personalized coaching specific to your situation.

Visit the website ***misskaykrizz.com*** for more information.

About the Author

Miss Kaykrizz is a Flight Attendant, Blogger and YouTuber.

She was a Flight Attendant in the Philippines for PAL Express for 3 years and an international flight attendant for a Middle East airline company for 3 years. She first created a blog where she detailed her experience with applying for the position of Flight Attendant for different airline companies in the Philippines, as well as international airlines that conducted recruitments in the Philippines. Those companies include Philippine Airlines, Cebu Pacific Air, Air Asia, PAL Express, Saudi Airlines, Qatar Airways, Emirates, Oman Air, and Air Nuigini. She applied to most of these companies more than once and got rejected for Qatar Airways for 8 times. She got accepted with Qatar Airways on her last try, but ultimately, her application was cancelled due to the airline requirements. After getting over the pain she immediately got accepted with another airline in the Middle East by applying all the learnings she gained from all the rejections.

The blog then became a YouTube Channel where initially she addresses many questions from her blog posts.

In college, she took up B.S. Nursing and is a Registered Nurse in 2009. Shortly after she worked as a customer service representative for Convergys and In-phone Sales Representative for Xlibris for a year. She founded the Miss Kaykrizz Facebook Group where she hosts a community of applicants who support each other in reaching their goals to become a Flight Attendant.

She also gives out a free monthly Hiring Alerts Email called the Miss Kaykrizz Newsletter which details the current airlines that are hiring in the Philippines every month.

Regarding other endeavors, she is very passionate about health and wellness, healing traumatic childhood wounds, spiritual awakening, travelling, puppies, financial literacy and entrepreneurship.

But above all these, Kaykrizz believes that her first call is to become the best version of herself, no matter what that may mean in the future.

For more information, log on to her website www.misskaykrizz.com or email her *kaykrizz@misskaykrizz.com*

Made in the USA
Middletown, DE
04 October 2021

49585711R00066